Contents

ABOUT THE AUTHOR

Sanjay Caines is a Computer Technician and businessman with very humble beginnings. Born on December 20th, 1980 to father Michael Caines, a locally popular mechanic/businessman, and Mother Phyllis Brookes, an office clerk, he was raised in an area of Basseterre called Mac Knight on the Caribbean Island of St. Kitts.

Sanjay's Primary Education started at George Moody Stuart School (Factory School). It was certainly the most prestigious private school at the time. His being there was made possible by his father's business, and it was just a stone's throw away from the sugar factory that was at the centre of the island economy then.

At an early age, Sanjay showed signs of a God-given writing talent by composing songs for a church group called 'Holy Vessels' while he attended the Basseterre Church of God. All throughout his youth, Sanjay wrote poems, mostly religious, and presented them at concerts, funerals and other special occasions. He also began to design pamphlets and tickets for these events, and crafted his poems on plaques by request. This helped to prepare Sanjay for larger business ventures.

He obtained a modest Secondary Education at the Basseterre Junior (now Washington Archibald) and Senior High Schools, passing five CXC subjects, including Mathematics and English. Sanjay also holds an ordinary level pass in English from the University of Cambridge, London (1998). Sanjay seemed earmarked to achieve greatness. His keen interest in science caused him to set his eyes on becoming a medical doctor.

Unfortunately, his father had migrated, and Sanjay was left to pursue his tertiary education on his own. He did not have the collateral to secure a student loan, and was unsuccessful in obtaining a sport scholarship, despite being full of potential in Lawn tennis and representing St. Kitts/Nevis in regional I.T.F tournaments.

None of these obstacles stopped him. He found his second God-given talent in Computer Science, with a focus on repairs. Family and friends soon realized that his ability to repair computers seemed to be genetically linked to his father's ability to fix cars.

Sanjay secured his first loan to establish his computer support business by fixing computers that a financial intuition had thrown out. They were returned to them upgraded, including sensitive data recovered.

Sanjay holds several computer-related certifications, and is currently C.E.O of Global Computer Franchise (G.C.F) and President of Youth Entrepreneurs and Professionals (Y.E.P).

Y.E.P also owns the publishing label YEPbook and is in the process of making the work of others available globally via **www.purposefulauthors.com**.

FOREWORD

This small collection of poems means quite a lot to me, due to the fact that I had written many more poems before, that were destroyed by hurricane. One thing is certain, though they may never be recovered physically or even by my own memory, the hearers at that particular moment in time were blessed. This generation needs some philosophical guidelines, as our societies are plunging into a 'state of convenience' that is at constant battle with our conscience.

Inspiration can come from the littlest of things, but which have the potential to reach and impact great kings. When this occurs, the seemingly unreal artistic utterances of poetry can find themselves a command away from reality.

There are many questions in life as they relate to life itself, death, success, religion, world powers, suffering and relationships, just to name a few. Whatever the question, there is no doubt that inspiration is the vital first step in influencing positive outcomes and perhaps getting closer to an answer. When the inspiration is shared successfully, each inspired person forms a greater force against the impossible, making it possible.

This generation has certainly lost the sense of collaboration. Consequentially, working together as a people of different races and religious beliefs, has now become impossible, and only inspiration can make it possible again.

This book is the consolidation of a locally-published book entitled "Using occasions to inspire generations", and is the most recent collection of my work, which is a deeper and more mature view of life's many situations. Now on the international scene, it is my hope to generate enough interest in my work that the inspired and adventurous souls the world over would be prompted to visit my home country of St. Kitts/ Nevis.

In this new global economy, one curious visit to a small island can mean investment and business opportunities that are mutually beneficial. In addition, there is a well known and established Citizenship By Investment Programme which seeks to secure the interests of potential investors via citizenship, property ownership and ongoing investment prospects.

We also boast an annual Music Festival that takes place at the ending of June, featuring international acts, and many vintage and exotic hotels and beaches that are worth experiencing. This is an opportune time to visit and have fun.

"Using Occasions to Inspire Generations" was an attempt to have inspirational work at the fingertips of both Ministers of Government and Religion, who are constantly called upon to console and provide comfort and inspiration in situations where they themselves would often need comfort as well.

The title, "Life's Questions" ought to catch the attention of many people, but my objective is not to answer the questions, but rather to begin the thought process necessary for readers to find their own answers and ultimately lead them to understand their purpose in life.

Collectively, these poems would not only inspire but challenge minds to expand the thought process, thus being more creative and productive.
Look at your world again. Try to see something you never saw, aspire to a height you never imagined. Think a thought you never thought possible. Be poetic, be bold, and be inspired to positively impact the world.

As you support this work, introduce it as a gift to your family, friends and loved ones. Each poem is available on hand-crafted plaques in various sizes that can be requested via the email sanjaycaines@hotmail.com.

I am also available for workshops, seminars and the public delivery of inspirational speeches and poems for any occasion. I enjoy and welcome the challenge of personalizing poems to meet your specific situation. Bookings can be done at www.sanjaycaines.com. It can be just one word in one line that provides the inspiration needed to move you and your loved ones to the next level in faith, success and destiny.

MANY THANKS TO...

Almighty God, my source of wisdom and continued inspiration.

My Manager and close friend, Ms. Empress Stanley (BSc Management Studies Hons U.W.I), who continues to be supportive.

Mr. Michael S. Blake for editorial insights, and endorsement.

Winston 'Zack' Nisbett (Cultural Preservationist & Curator of the International House Museum) for preserving two poems.

The Labour Spokesman for allowing me to search their archive for some of my poems that were published more than a decade ago.

The St. Kitts Tourism Authority and Nevis Tourism Authority, for high quality images.

St. Kitts Scenic Railway, and other tourism attractions for collaborating.

Willett's Photo Studio, for cover design.

D'Jorn Dias, for his original artwork.

The Ministry of Education for their support.

All the people who made the launch of this book an event to remember.

Life's Questions

What does life really entail?

What determines if a man wins or fails?

Why poverty? Why live unhealthy, unclean?

Are resources in abundance only for kings and queens?

What is money? Man's God-made asset of metal and paper?

Be careful with earthly things, they have wings. Gone in a vapor!

How valuable is money compared to one's health?

Can it be regained by the entire world's wealth?

Where are true friends when you are really in need?

When your barns are full, they appear and feed.

How many rivers run to the ocean?

When love is one-sided, is there really a portion?

Now, all of your problems are gone, your face is beaming!

Hello! Wake up, you are either in another world, or dreaming.

Welcome to reality! Look for solutions, problems are always there.

STOP! Worry no more; someone really does care.

Before the lens of your eyes go dim,

Call on Him!

Who is this being? I don't want to be religiously wrong

He answers life's questions in prophesy, in poetry, and in song.

What does God require of me?

What does God require of me?

This question should be on the minds of those seeking to be free

First He requires salvation from the shackles of sin

Not a brand of religion but sealed with his power within

When your spirit is broken by trials and pain

From the dark clouds of failure, he releases the latter rain

He require you to use your talents for the world to see

He has equipped you for a life of purpose and prosperity

What does God require of me?

Vigilance, patience and the grace to manifest my vision with clarity

He requires me to use the weapons of prayer and praise

Raising the standard, always ready for the next phase

What does God require of us?

Unity, collaboration and consensus

Together, purposefully to do His will

The enemy plans to conquer. His strategy: steal, destroy and kill.

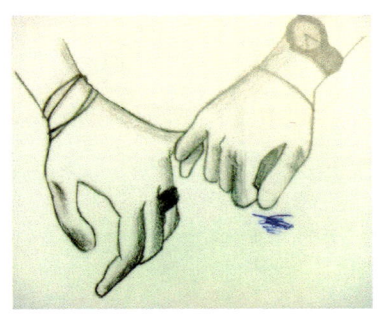

Is there a God?

"I am an atheist!" I heard an elderly lady say.

This surprised me. I planned to challenge her belief someday.

My country is tiny, but churches of all sorts fill.

Regrettably, very few want to do God's will.

What I found by far most funny,

Most insisting that God needs our money!

And even more embarrassing, a total disaster!

The Parish girls sugar, the Parish Pastor?

I thought, people do have a basis to question if this is real;

Especially when Jesus is packaged with Easter eggs and Santa

Clause, fairytale?

My job just got a little complicated:

On what basis, can I convince this atheist, when being debated?

"Take me to church", has become the biggest laugh,

As doctrines are many, but the Book does NOT support half.

The day finally came, the meeting was set,

There in a garden behind an old café we met.

"Lad," she said. "This is what I believe in:

The creation, not perversion, not sin."

Looking around, I almost agree -

Nature preaches its own doctrines of peace, love and liberty.

I saw lizards, butterflies, birds and ants,

Wearing no suits and ties and making no baseless rants.

I asked, quite politely, "Who created all this?"

"Of course," she replied, "it evolved from the abyss."

Could it be that mankind is so corrupted, that people are just ashamed

To admit that an Intelligent Being created us, to honor His name?

"Look" I insisted, "Let's not focus on the clowns in religious gowns."

Then there was silence, our ears surrendered to nature's sounds

The debate ended, nature's tune echo abroad:

"There is a Creator, there is a God!"

Which Church Do I Attend?

This is a big question. From a deep thought, it came

YAHWEH; Jehovah; Yahshua; Jesus' name?

How can I tell a true pastor?

Which denomination would get me to heaven, or hell, faster?

Life, as we know it, will someday pass;

Amidst many schools of thought, which has the right class?

Of all life's questions, the impact of this is eternal.

Why go with the flow? Listen to voices internal.

The study of religious history, full of insight,

Shows Jesus, transliterated. That's the plight.

Religion proposes to honour His name,

But in blatant contradiction, ignores the teachings of same.

Did I answer the question? I thought that I already did.

Know God's Spirit and voice for yourself. That is your best bid.

Find out the gifts He gave you, use them for His will.

Religious folks boast of church membership, knowing their folly, be

still.

Many serve a God they think is deaf and blind.

Imagine the shock on judgment day, to find

The roll is called up yonder! NO Denomination singled out!

What have you done with the works of your hands; the words of

your mouth?

Brother, sister, find your God before you find a church,

Or else the blind will lead blind, forever in search,

Of simple truths foolishly debated.

Religion makes finding God, complicated.

What If?

It feels like a drought defeated by rain.

Wished there was no doubt, released from pain.

The birds, they fly, and fishes do swim.

As the years roll by, man's vision grows dim.

What if you could see without natural eyes,

And no ears needed to hear the underprivileged cries?

What if Jesus wasn't abused by religion,

And man listened to the still voice before decision?

What if I remained uninspired - NO poetic words!

No wisdom, no guidance like Shepherds and herds?

What if I refused to do the best I can,

To uplift and liberate my fellow man?

Inspired again! Like an artist on a masterpiece,

Using colours of war to portray an image of peace.

What if I was not liberated, but mentally enslaved?

I could only be happier buried in a grave.

What if this poem never came to an end,

And all of life's questions we could comprehend?

What if you hear a sound? Not with your natural ear-

Arise my brother! Victory is near!

What is your purpose?

Focus. What is your purpose on earth?

Of all life's questions, this has the greatest worth.

Through purity and righteousness comes the power to serve;

All of God's creation, everyone deserves;

To find his God-ordained purpose,

Not a religion that misleads and condemns us.

Father a carpenter, Mother yielded to God's plan:

Were these the right conditions for a Saviour to come to man?

Of course, there were Princes, Queens and Kings,

But the carnal mind is confused by heavenly things!

No mortal is perfect; we all have made at least one mistake!

Who made you judge, to condemn and control us, for religion's

sake?

Remember Job? Stripped from his comfort zone!

A praying and upright man, but purpose-tested for everything he

owned

Remember Jonah? From purpose he tried to run;

Thrown overboard, transported by a fish; Was that fun?

Is your life less than perfect? Welcome to the crew!

Not to criticize, but to establish faith and prosper you.

Focus! What is your purpose in life?

Certainly not to be poor, sick, comfortless, and living in strife!

Are You a Leader?

Crisis! Shortage of leaders, where are they?

Focus misguided, power, position, pay!

Character, where does it hide nowadays

Seems like only the vile attracts man's praise

Oh! Ok, he is educated. No criminal record

The perfect candidate to commit fraud

Siren, guns, police at the door

Ready to pin the crime on the weak, the poor

Imagine leadership, faith love and peace

Sacrificed for corruption, war and wickedness increase

A generation pursuing perfection, an unblemished reputation

is for what all strive

But in reality there is none good, no perfect man alive.

Leaders emerge from the illusion and confusion with confidence

That their expertise and experience highlight their competence

The stage is set, the waiting audience is attentive

Are you a leader? Say something, do something, inspire men to

live.

What is Love

Hurry up! Say what love is

I have tried to answer this ancient quiz

Don't get religious and say love is God

Heard that before, that is too broad

This person I am dating does she love me

Can I identify it in her personality?

Hold up! Rewind

Love can be very hard or very easy to find

It depends on where you look

Your perceptions and your faith in the Book

What do you want out of life?

Success? Children? A husband or wife?

Then love inspires you.

Slows you down to notice the evening dew

But if every fish comes by, you are ready to swim

Hello bitterness, the chances of finding love – slim

You with peddle to the floor, fast car, how long will you last?

Love is waiting at your door – but you just passed

There He is, with faith and hope, ready to greet you

Are you there, ready for answers? Love Himself will meet you

Is There a Good in Goodbye?

There is obviously a good in the word 'goodbye'

It humbles us to the point that we have to cry

Unaware at that moment, tears are a language God fully under-

stands

And crying, NOT fighting separated a boy from a man.

So let them fall, yes, the tears

They are washing away the pain of those hurtful years

And clearing your vision so you could see

The good in 'goodbye' is being set free

Free from those emotions that whispered in your ear

'Goodbye' is the saddest word you will ever hear

Free from the thought that separation is always bad

Reject this world, serve your creator, you will be glad

Free to reflect on your condition before

You saw 'goodbye' as the key that opened the door

To your dreams, desires and blessings in excess

Now your sorrows are exchanged for peace and happiness

Deeper Still

Think a thought: is it wholesome? Is it God's will?

Wait, expand on that thought, Deeper Still!

Where is it leading? Are there any signs that need heeding?

What forces have you invoked? Demons or angels pleading?

It's your thought, coming from your mind!

It's also a simple test, your master to find.

Where did that thought come from? Who is in control

Of your mind body and soul?

Hold that thought! Though it is your right to express

Your allegiance to light or darkness,

There is still time to reshuffle your deck.

Would your thought expressed, perceive a joker or intellect?

Are you ready to express

That powerful, wise thought of righteousness?

If not, test the spirit, relax, chill.

There is one, always echoing, deeper still.

Perception

Look all around. There is the perception to perceive,

Things portrayed by scientists and scholars. Do you believe?

Do you feel the push of social norm – perception,

Defined technically as personal deception?

In essence we have been prescribed a pill to swallow

Think! 'Rethink'! Are you ill? Why follow?

Let us perceive for a moment that some things are true:

Leaders really love people, and your neighbours do love you.

A poet's pen will never express words of depression;

Our communities should be overflowing with compassion

Eyes open? While we perceive things are so,

The reality is ill will and animosity flow

From our leaders, impacting the smallest child,

This is no perception. Upon reflection, a generation has gone wild!

Even without recognition, never give up, you will achieve

Challenge your cognition,

Make real your vision….Perceive!

Society

I am a little confused,

Yet, fascinated and amused.

So many emotions,

So many schools of thoughts trying to own my devotions.

I am a nice guy, don't you think?

I don't smoke, but I need a drink!

Nothing heavy, something light,

My thoughts are heavy enough trying to win this fight.

Can I win, or am I bound to lose?

Can society judge sin, or the philosophies I choose?

What a pity!

Confrontation! Things not looking pretty

I was created with the purpose of being free and enjoying God's

earth,

But society, hijacked by evil men, laid claim on my life since

birth.

"Black boy, an education is the way to success,

Leave your brothers behind in the mess."

Was not anticipated, slavery reincarnated.

Saddled with debt, the goals of the capitalists are met.

Now I am educated, but do I have the means or the brains,

To break FREE, from these financial and mental chains?

A New Age Slavery

Pass me that History book;

Let the eyes of a poet take a look:

Shipped from Africa to the Caribbean shore-

Beaten, Bruised, Enslaved; Poor,

Working hard daily to secure bread.

In the evening, a blanket only as a bed.

Rise and shine! Another day is here:

A cup of tea, loaf of bread, the master, fear,

Hot sun, sweating, sorrow, pain.

It's evening; afraid to dream of tomorrow.

Injustice again!

Fast forward: it's after 1838, Emancipation!

But why are my eyes still seeing an enslaved generation?

That reminds me; slavery, or employment?

Remember we are free - to pay utilities and rent!

Free to think of, and achieve our goals

NO masters, only bosses to torment our souls.

Month end; where is the paid wage?

Need more proof? Slavery disguised in a new age.

Full Emancipation

FREEDOM! Caribbean history records was granted in 1838

And our ancestors were free to leave the estates

Ex-slaves in the larger territories held freedom in their hands

And tasted destiny by squatting on crown lands

Ex-slaves in the smaller territories knew in their heart

Freedom was granted, but only in part

They had to work for low wages to buy food and pay rent

Slavery was reintroduced in the form of 'employment'

Even now after two centuries have passed

The 'free' still wait for King's dream to manifest, 'free at last!'

Freedom must transcend the dreams of Martin Luther King

And be manifested in our daily lives as a tangible thing

That we can see it every morning as we open our eyes

As the power that sustains us, and causes us to rise

By faith beyond the boundaries that are set by man

Who says we can't, but freedom hears, 'we can'

Swims like fishes, flies like the birds

Freedom is already granted by the power of God's words

When your souls and spirits are reclaimed by salvation,

Only then would you understand the feeling. Full Emancipation!

The Pen

The pen is most powerful. Wars start and end;

With its accomplice, paper, many philosophies they defend.

Their relevance technology tried to overthrow

Emails, word processing, pen and paper? NO!

The pen has been through battles, whited out, covered clean -

But the pen, also upgraded, now can write on screen!

Technology is amazing but more so the divine.

I was born with pen hands-on, these fingers of mine.

It's an ancient saying, "The pen's mightier than the sword."

With little mention of paper derived from board.

Together, they have done more than doodle and spills.

Many authorizations, signatures, passage of parliamentary bills.

Billions of X's and √'s by Teachers in schools,

And have determined, via exams, scholars from fools.

But the greatest achievements of these ancient friends

Are words of inspiration, expressed with paper and pens.

The Band Plays On...

Life is like a band with many tunes,

Playing always throughout the new moons.

The death of a loved one is never one's will;

The band, missing an instrument, plays on still.

Now the tune will never be the same,

But we must continue to trust in Jesus' name.

He is the maestro who controls every note.

Calm your emotions; our saviour is on the boat.

Cling to that faint thought of hope;

Listen to the band again, now you can cope.

The band plays on, and your tune is ever clear,

The band of life plays what you INSIST to hear.

Don't be sorrowful; don't give in to your pain,

Look for sunshine, although you hear rain

The band plays on, leaving your countenance sad;

Now the verse is done; your spirit is suddenly glad.

You are now revived by the words of the chorus:

"Our Creator knows all, and He will comfort us".

All Things

Dedicated with love to all those who are in distress,
Due to calamities such as imprisonment, bereavement and sick-
ness,
Hoping that you will appreciate the joy this poem brings
By turning your tears into smiles as you understand the phrase,
'All Things'.

All things work together to fulfill our destiny
Although sometimes it's hard for our natural eyes to see,
Especially in the midst of our pain and misery;
The fervent prayer of our hearts is to be set free.
Suddenly, a voice echoes from out of the blue:
"Fear not my child, I will not forsake you".

Then the darkness surrenders to a beam of light -
Now joy is ours, because we endured the night
At last, the pain is gone, and the victory is won.
"Daddy, I feel sick," Oh my, another test has begun!

It must be the will of God for mortals to meet with triumph and
distress,
And amidst them both declare: "I am blessed,"
Recognizing that there will be sunny days and stormy weather,
A smile comes from knowing 'All Things' are working together.
As I opened the Book to read about the experiences of Job,
My thoughts were shifted in an instant to Joseph's colourful robe.

Both men struggled but achieved good success.
They did not curse God in their time of distress.

At last, the mysterious tune that the carefree bird sings,

Has been revealed to all mankind,

"All Things."

A Father Leads

A father leads over mountainous terrains

When the sun is scorching, when there are torrent rains

Having no control over the natural elements

Yet, can, through wisdom, turn criticism into compliments

A father leads his wife and children, in times of plenty and need

Admonishing them to be patient, and not to be overcome by greed

He leads to perfection while trying to attain the same

Looking at his reflection he can recognize both triumph and shame

A father leads when there is the feeling to give up

In the midst of a desert, can drink water from faith's cup

Giving hope to his family while he himself may be sad

Broken by sorrows, but still can make them glad

He rises, he falls, and he walks, and at times has to speed

All the while driven by the word,

'LEAD'.

Getting Old

Ok, you are getting old

But you probably did not recognize it, until you were told.

You look great!

Is it because of the healthy things that you ate?

Every year, it's the same old,

Getting old…..

But look again, you would find the treasure

You are not just aging, but increasing in measure

Whatever your age,

It's like the book of your life just concluded another page.

And you can be excited again; set another goal

Don't just think… 'I'm getting old'

No, age is not just a vehicle to take you to destination death!

It is a chance to live and never regret,

Because the dreaded word, AGE

Is the reason for you to enjoy the next stage.

Come to my homeland!

MacKnight! Located in historic Basseterre, There I was raised;

Memories of an average childhood, God, and parents praised

Permit me to paint an image, with a poetic brush:

SKN - exotic, vintage, compared to big city rush.

Even here, politics and religion, deep roots -

Generation to generation, seeking to uncover truths.

A peculiar people, unique in many ways.

Relax while on the Scenic Railway or tour the island, you will be amazed.

Projects not yet conceived, to be facilitated by former sugar lands.

Ready to invest? Do so as your pocket demands.

Off to the South-East, you will find Christophe Harbour and scenery divine!

Hotels, beaches, residential homes of every kind.

Let's stop for a Marriott breakfast - don't be late!

Buffet style, local delicacies galore; take another plate.

Is there such a thing as poetic cheating?

Hope I am not overly inspired, here now eating.

Through a large window, I see birds playing.

A pale blue sky and coconut trees, swaying.

The breeze from the Atlantic Ocean will blow away your gloom.

I am looking at an empty chair; Book a room?

Travel back to the history rich town by taxi, or free will.

Stop! Beyond the Newtown shoreline, Port Zante,

Duty free shopping Thrill!

Be prepared to fill both your face and suitcase.

YES! Food again with arts and crafts, Amina Craft Market is the place.

One vendor in particular, is sure to reignite life's spark

when you see what he has made, craftsman Mark.

So much to see, so little time in the day.

And you have not explored Brimstone Hill or the sister island Nevis, STAY!

I may have a way with words, but you must understand

this is a simple plea, though creatively

Come to my homeland

Nevis Nice!

St. Kitts is attractive, but Nevis is Nice!

Can this simple overused word describe a paradise?

Strangely, it does. Even the most complicated word
would be insignificant

To describe a treasure, Nevis. It is both unique and
magnificent.

The birthplace of Alexander Hamilton; lavish home of
the Four Season Resort;

Perfect place to live, and to vacation; with interesting
activities of all sorts.

The Ferry is ready to travel the ocean. Pack! Prepare!
Is city life a bit frustrating? Tranquility is waiting there!

She is called 'Queen City'! Confident, like a woman
who takes control,

And delivers the goods while she remains pretty,
completely captivating your soul.

Come! Yes, you! The Botanical Garden awaits.

Feeling sentimental? Relax in plantation inns that
were former Sugar Estates.

Walk, or swim on Pinney's Beach. Sample the
famous drink, Bumble Bee.

This is it - authentic Caribbean sun, sand and sea.

Rejuvenate your body at the mineral springs located in Bath;

Join the many who have visited. Nevis lives forever in their heart.

Yes, Nevis Nice!!

The Power of a Dream

Relax, close your eyes and begin to dream.
Surprised? Things are no longer how they seemed.

You were sick, now you are healed,

You were hungry, now you have a meal.

You were sad, and filled with despair

Now you are glad, and filled with cheer.

You were poor, now you are rich,

You wish it was a permanent switch.

Wait! Before you awake, dream once more,

Like Joseph, your oppressors you must ignore

Hold fast to your dreams and you will achieve.

Let people think, say and do, while you believe

That your pit is God's preparation for the palace.

When you arrive, in your heart there will be no malice.

Now you can serve your brothers whose intentions were to kill,

With a smile, recognizing the brilliance of the Master's will.

If, on a cloudy day, you can see the sun's beam,
With keys of faith, you have unlocked the power of a dream.
Now you can live, yes you can forgive;
Let us work together, as a team.

The Little Things

Look at the leaves dancing in the trees,

As they move to the rhythm of the breeze

And the birds spreading their wings while flying

Never thinking about sickness or dying

Look at the moon glowing in the night,

Reflecting the splendor of the sunlight

And the clouds relaxing in the sky

Releasing rain when the earth is dry

Though Zacchaeus was small, he climbed a tree,

And shouted, "Lord, have mercy on me!"

Josiah was eight when he began to reign

And the principles of God he did maintain

From even the children God has ordered praise,

In preparation for leadership in the last days

From a little meal Jesus fed a multitude

Five loaves of bread and two fishes provided enough food

It is these little things that build great faith,

When we consider them we will appreciate

The miracle of life,

The foolishness of strife,

And the wisdom of Kings, in little things.

The Word of the Hour

It's the night before; my name is up to preach
Souls to deliver, encouragement to give, conscience to reach
The Devil like a roaring lion seeks whom he may devour
His plans exposed, it's almost revealed! The word of the hour

There in quietness I wait,
Heart in tune with empty cup and plate
I see a vision of the faces in the congregation
With many questions concerning different situations
My lips sealed shut, nothing in mind to say
Still waiting for God's Spirit to have his way

Then came the release, a burst of revelation
Flowing like a river to a thirsty congregation
Spiritual questions that evoked deep thought
Are we guided by God's spirit as we ought?
Are we living to eat, or eating to live?
Is it really easier to move mountains than to forgive?
Why have we abandoned faith and truth?
For traditions, the love of money, the root.

Religion indoctrinates and gives a false sense of liberty
Get out, get in connection with your Creator. You are FREE!

Our Rights Remain

We are all born free and equal. Don't discriminate!

We all have the right to life. STOP the hate!

No slavery, No torture. We have rights, no matter where we roam;

Equal before the law, in foreign lands or home.

Our rights are protected by law: no unfair detainment;

The right to trial; Innocent until proven guilty; No unjust punish-

ment.

We have a right to privacy, and the freedom to move to a place of

tranquility;

A safe place to live; a nationality.

The right to marriage, Family and our own things.

The right to think and express those thoughts before queens and

kings.

The right to public assembly, democracy and social security;

Workers' Rights; the right to play; food and shelter for all humani-

ty.

The right to Education and Copyright, in a world fair and free!

Yes, we have Rights! But also a sacred responsibility.

Leaders, if ever you conceive policies that are inhumane,

Remember, we are Human; and pledge to respect others.

But our Rights remain!

The Vanity of Youth

Strength of youth is in that innocent face,
Determined to be first, no matter the race.

Wisdom of youth is in the faith to believe,
Our dreams and noble goals we will achieve.

We suffer for the things that we do wrong,
But resilience will teach us to be strong.

Zeal of youth will drive us speedily ahead.
Let's reflect on what our parents have said.

The privilege of youth must not be abused.
Experienced once, no one gets to choose.

King Solomon taught many lessons to youth,
Such as obedience, and the importance of truth

Admonishing now, rather than later,
To remember and worship our Creator.

The vanity of youth will soon pass us by;
You are not too young to serve the Most High,

So make good use of your youth like Hezekiah.
You will not be denied your heart's desire

When your teeth are gone and eyes are dim.
God will reward you for serving Him.

Creative, Industrious Youth!

Youth at risk!

Are you one? How do you feel?
Misunderstood, judged, imprisoned, behind bars of cold steel.
Social and religious policies ofer no room; no place.
Rise up! Help yourself! Wipe your tears from your face!
You are not alone; your Creator is near,
Your wounds to heal, your prayers to hear
. Discrimination; segregation; "I am better than you!"
Are these the real objectives? Masked by tie and jacket, too?

Politician!

Are you one? How do you feel?
What is your mission? Time and truth will reveal.
Any solid plans for the Nation? Besides tax heavy legislation.

Young men criminals, young women's body for a price
The state ofers Education, the Church - Salvation
through Jesus Christ.
What is the solution? Few families at home!
Mother's distressed, children unattended while fathers roam.
Can you hear the underprivileged cry?
Or are you busy building a castle in the sky?

Creative, Industrious Youth!

Are you one? How do you feel?
Your fellow men are uninspired, without conviction and zeal.
You have caught the vision and made the decision to lead.
You are responsible. Yes, you, take heed!

Collaborate, educate, motivate and share the truth.
Unleash your potential; grow, by thinking deeper than the
average youth.

Mental evolution is the solution. This is my plea;
Enslaved by the system? Invent, use your talents, and break
FREE!

Through Your Eyes

I saw through your eyes, just as you wondered if I would ever see..

Emotions locked up inside of you for me.
It was during one of those speechless and seemingly pointless stare

That I saw you, hoping that I had the power to hear
Voices of your heart, the rhythm of your soul,
The melody of which remains untold.

I was surprised, but what is to be, will be
The power of your captive thoughts inspires me.

Probably told you I was poetic, but never in my wildest dream,
Would I see through your eyes, a vision of us as a family,
A purpose driven team.

Through your eyes, your virtue can be seen.
It resembles the beauty and strength of a queen.
From your soul, yes, the rhythm I have heard,
And voices of your heart, without saying a word.
We are becoming us, strengthened by every test.
Now our journey has started, I commit to you my friend

My future, my EMPRESS.

My First Love

What is love? I honestly do not know

But each time I see her, there is a smile, a glow

Stop the poem! There she is, emotions now beaming

Does it matter, if I am awake or dreaming?

I am in love but my lover is yet to know

Hush. Don't say a word, my cover to blow

Eyes open, flat on my back in my bed, awake

Don't judge me. I am still trying to believe her love for me is not

fake

Guess what? I will see her at work today

And I have already rehearsed a million rhymes to say

There she is just sitting alone

It's my time to face reality or send a text to her phone

But I don't know her number

I will ask her while I take my slumber

There I have more control, I am the director and we are the actors

Lights, camera, time to set the scene and tweak the factors

I won't make it too long, the highlight is the ending

She really likes me but she is just pretending

Another day, face down, searching, what do I find?

Reality is painful; the pleasure of my first love is all in my mind

The Vow

Here we are, our time is now

To make, and never to break, the vow.

It is sacred, beyond the realm of man.

By faith we pledge to remain hand in hand.

Even the toughest trials, are no excuse!

This bond to break, this knot to loose

We are now one in spirit and soul

Perfecting love, as time unfold.

You and I no longer exist

We commit to us, sealed with a kiss,

In the presence of both God and man.

We are fulfilling a divine master plan.

The obstacles are many, true friends few.

Each overcast day, will surrender to blue.

Surely, we have impacted our nation

Fulfilling God's will in our generation

Standing here and now, we take the vow!

Us and God, we will make it, somehow.....

Mother

Mother, are words sufficient enough to say,

How much you mean to me every day?

Of course not, but they are trying their best,

That is why I cherish the opportunity to express

The gratitude of my life resulting from yours.

And to confess, I hated you a little, when you gave me chores.

When I was a little child you did what you could,

And for all your efforts, the whole of humanity should

Give a passing grade to mothers, who constantly have ends to

meet,

While covering it well behind the strategic showing of teeth.

Your smile is extra beautiful and only now I know why;

It seems to wipe away the memories of the times you had to cry;

As you fought against the forces that are set against a mother and

child,

Rich or poor, educated or not, you positioned yourself, you toiled

On a journey that's filled with both pleasure and pain.

Look at me, I am grateful…were your efforts in vain?

NEVER, Mother!!

Graduate

Our time has come through hard work and faith

From trials to triumph we graduate

We know more now than when we started

Due to the prolific knowledge this institution has imparted

This gratitude is not directed to the walls

But to the teachers and lecturers who answered the calls

From deep inspiration, deep resolve

Committing to the challenge, problems to solve

It's our time to drink from the hottest cup of tea

To reflect and think of our responsibility

To God, ourselves, our families, and this Institution

For bringing our dreams closer to fruition

We are a class of purpose, a class who appreciate

The role each has played for us, to Graduate.

The Spirit of Christmas

The Spirit of Christmas is in the air,

Let's make haste to show that we care.

Strange isn't it? We let the whole year pass -

Perhaps we have saved the best for last!

The spirit of Christmas is suddenly set free;

The children's hearts are filled with glee.

But the Saviour brings a different message to town:

"Love your neighbour all year round."

Spirit of Christmas, please stay a while;

Don't erase the hugs and the smiles.

Linger over us the whole year through,

Turning all of our grey skies blue.

The world will be better, and wars will cease

If only we yield to the Prince of Peace

Spirit of Christmas, hear our heart's prayer:

"Stay with us all throughout the year."

Christmas Deception

The Christmas deception, is indeed a sight to see:
Flashing lights, mistletoe, goodwill, and revelry!
Tiny tots are excited, but most gullible,
Doctrines of Satan, promoted infallible.
It scares me, even angers my soul!
Are these the children we expect, to show respect, as they grow old?
Is this the basis on which we live in a society gone wild?
And perhaps, lay blame on the God-Child?

After all, it's His birthday, He is the reason!
You deceive, commercialize and legalize sin for this season.
Do these words seem unreal? Give yourself a pinch,
If you are inspired, I won't regret being called the 'Grinch.'
Celebrating Christmas, is destructive enough on its own;
Mixed with carnival, the effects are hardly outgrown.

Don't get vexed,
If you perceive that I am out of context.

Examine what I am saying,
Listen to the songs that are playing.
"I believe in Santa Clause", "Away in a manger",
Can generations yet unborn be in more danger?
Exactly what is our culture, can anyone tell?
Are we advertising heaven, while securing a Nation of hell?

The Christmas tree and others are Biblical paganism
(Jeremiah 10 vs. 1-5)
Would your Jesus celebrate idolatry, gluttony and materialism?

No End

This is it! Or is it? My friend

We have met philosophically - The End

Very sad, don't you think?
The most precious of time, gone in a wink
Were you inspired? Were you blessed?
My purpose is to position you for success

Were your life's questions placed into perspective?
The answers are already there, revealed as you purposefully live

The Creator is never in a rush, He has the master plan
And time is not an issue, it responds to His command
But for us mere mortals, just tasting the spirit realm
Let's examine our lives, who is at the helm?

If you have allowed your mind to think deeper, obstacles transcend
You will find that the impact of your influence really has no end.

**Visit www.sanjaycaines.com
for more information**

www.globalcomputerfranchise.com

Affiliated with:

This book was made possible by the support of
Youth Entrepreneurs and Professionals

1-305-381-1040 U.S.A/International
Nevis Street, Basseterre
St. Kitts

Made in the USA
Charleston, SC
22 July 2016